dedicated to Hamish Fulton – *clouds are like walks, they come and go*

www.whitepeak-darkpeak.co.uk
www.re-place.co.uk
www.alecfinlay.com

white peak | dark peak

an audio-visual word-map of
The Peak District National Park

Alec Finlay

with
Ann Atkinson
Tony Baker
David Cobb
David Gilbert
Rebecca Hall
Alan Halsey
Hamish Ironside
Judy Kendall
Martin Lucas
India McKellar
Geraldine Monk
Peter Riley
Mark Rutter
John Sewell
Andrew Shimield
Caroline Smith
Ian Storr
David Troupes
Laura Watts
River Wolton

field-recordings | Bevis Bowden

renga readings | John Sewell

typography | Alec Finlay & StudioLR

morning star | Derbyshire Arts Development Group | 2010

skylines

each poet is a view

walking the skyline always changes

without outline there is no shape

brooks to walk to, rivers to walk along

a poem is an open fold

a poem is a niche

this is our poem Tom Tom

less than the whole dale gets in the poem

our views won't replace your views

the signpost's not the footpath

the tors cast stone as celebrity

next time *you* walk this

new thoughts, old paths; old paths, new thoughts

a walk does the eyes good, like a poem does the mind

nature is the cone, the cube and the Peak (after Cezanne)

speculating beyond land that's private or public

sunbathing, mountaineering: pursuits have to be invented

hikes and haiku extend the mind, bending habits into particulars

hill-farming is a colloquium of specialisms

each car has an A–Z torn on the page-spread for home

definitions

*poem:* line in time

*circle poem:* arc in time

*horizon:* line in space

*skyline:* earth drawn line

*peak:* line in dialect

*audio:* line that fades as it is drawn

*view:* point

*poet:* view

*reader:* viewer

*map:* poem (arranged NSEW)

*haiku:* glass marble

*renga:* glass bead necklace

*QR:* kanji barcode

*letterbox:* poem-cache, ink stash

*river:* flower

*mist:* tippex

*dale:* V-vale

*tor:* headline

*sun:* make a day of it

*rain:* are you coming too?

*rainbow:* meet you in the middle

letterboxing & circle poems

letterbox poems are found on the way

the places in-between letterboxes are also poems

every letterbox thinks it is the centre of the world

leave an ink pad fresher than you found it

rubber stamp poems always leave an impression

for every letterbox there is a guide and a keeper

always drill a hole in the bottom of your letterbox, or make sure that your poem can float

in letterboxing the laws of poetry and property sometimes conflict

ink should always be pure black

the perennial moral dilemma: how far to park your car from the poem

letterbox poetry sees into the wood and through the trees

direction in a circle poem is not marked in terms of fixed points, yet the poems do often have poles

circle poems favour rhythm over syntax

a circle poem knows that ends can be beginnings and beginnings ends

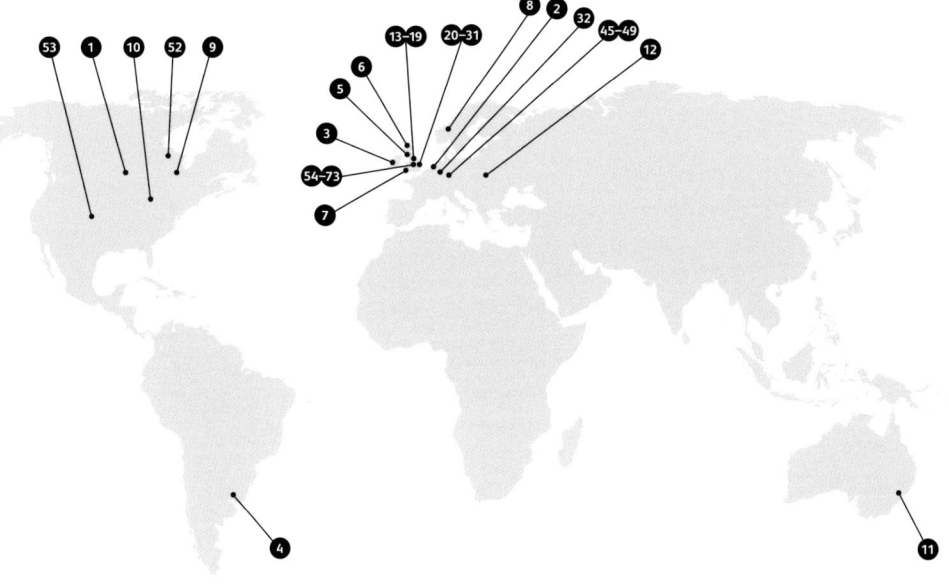

white peak | dark peak
WWLB054 – 073

worldwiderubberstampletterboxcirclepoem
*www.alecfinlay.com/letterbox*

P
A
T
H
S

innumerable branching trails
bright green ribbons
sunken hollows
ancient packways radiating across directionless moorlands
signposted rights of way
shady woodland tracks
paved pathways
Roman Roads
narrow thorn-banked lanes
rutted bridleways
sheep trods
step-in-step stepping stones
crooked branching roads

The following poems are not included in the audio

DRYSTONE

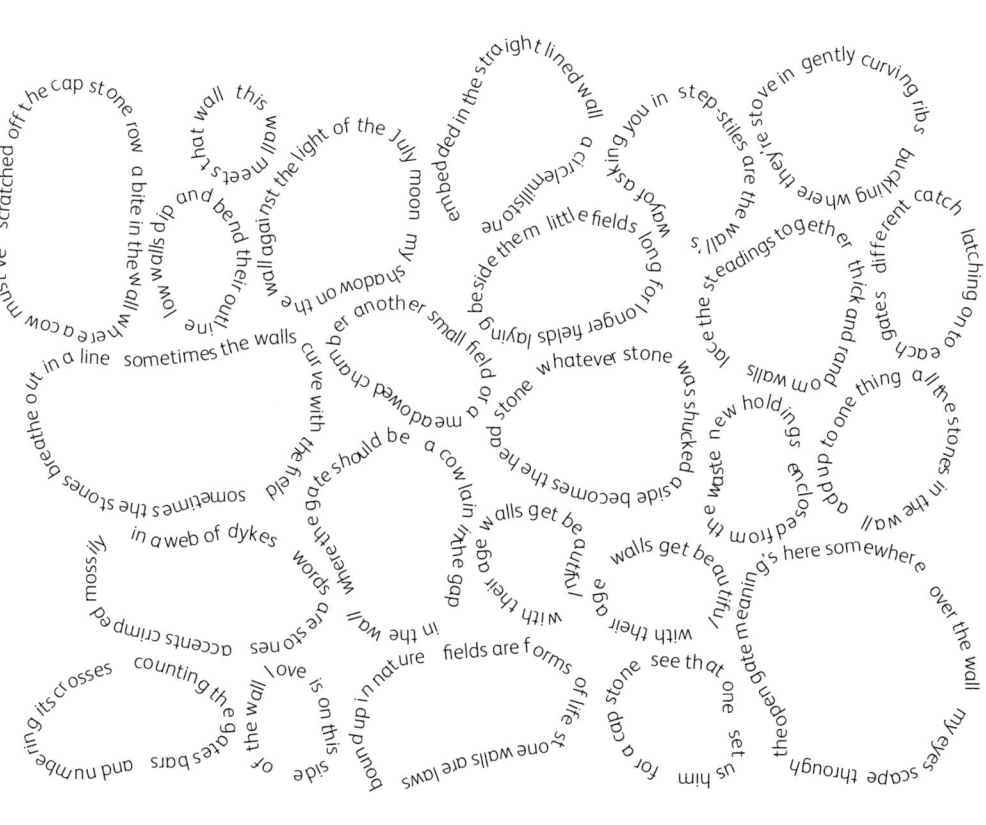

PEAKSCENE

    it's flinkerin'
      wi' snow
        up in the white peak

    the walking season's open
      when the ice cream van
        parks at Burbage North

    eye colours
      sky colours
        out the window


    free hot spot
      wi-fi at the café
        right by the stocks
*Chapel-en-le-Frith*

    reaching for my coat
      there's really no need
        for the weather forecast

    if it was a bit lower
      this stile
        could be furniture


    Casey's Stores
      yellow tea-cakes are soft
        and HUGE
*Great Longstone*

    wet and wind from the east
      High Peak Weather
        with CLEARVIEW WINDOWS

    a shivering clump of ash
      picks out the lost circle
        of the old low


    sat on the burial mound
      chatting about
        Michael Jackson's funeral
*Gib Hill*

    supping ale
      brewed in an owl
        roost

    bedded on the hill
      up in the sky
        taken out by the rain


    blown outside in-
      side any-
        way the wind bends

    a dusting of snow
      picks out
        the ancient field boundaries

    we built our homes
      along ledges and drove
        paths over slanting shelves
*Matlock*


    India's got one bike
      for dark
        another for white

    Hamps' pebbly-bed
      is a jar dry of water
        sloes and shady air
*Hamps Valley*

    Lord lead us
      into the wilderness
        on Sundays & Bank Holidays

# HAIKU

the good life's in Black's
   windowful of apparels
      & appurtenances

another turning missed
   engrossed in hill
      names on the map

smell something burning
   just the sun bumping
      along its solar minimum


ramblers from Manchester (CP)
   from Sheffield (ILP)
      fought each other in Spain

our headlights turn on
   scouts peeing
      in the bushes

sunken sided
   the lane leans
      in a natural apse
*Birchover Lane*


we drive
   until we arrive
      at a sign

night-driving over-
   head the trees
      meet up

between Bull & Eagle Tor
   the river swathes
      into a puthering spate


the bridge's 3
   eye slits peep
      at the flood
*Ashford in the Water (27.10.98)*

split gritstone slates
   pegged with oak
      weigh the rooves low pitch

look, everyone can forget
   what age they are
      (3,000, 4,000, 5,000 BC)
*Arbor Low*


climbers diss routes
   in the pub –
      Joe Brown's excepted

the roadsides
   windbreak trees
      held on the angle

where else
   would a mass trespass
      begin on a cricket pitch?
*Hayfield Village, 1932*


pignut & campion
   brush the length
      of the car

sometimes I fall in love
   with a name –
      Manifold

bolts, rotting slings & rusty pegs
   Body Machine contrives
      cliff into climbing wall
*Body Machine, route on Shining Tor*
*pioneered by Ron Fawcett, May 1984*

F
L
O
R
A

    you're pretty, so what!
        what for barren strawberry?
           yes but you are pretty
*On scree by the Dove near the gate*
*halfway down/up Wolfscote Dale*

    spikelets bend delicate
        floating wood-millet
           light over the ground

    flat grasses
        swivel their blades
           in the breeze

    nettles with flowers aren't
        nettles as is
           proven by touch

    after a good burn
        there's more bounce
           in the heather
*Beeley Moor, next to the*
*ice cream van station, and*
*northwards to Scotland*

    straggly chickweed
        lights out
           under the hedge
*Around the barn where Ted had*
*mucked out, on the lower side of*
*Winster Main St., 1990*

    burdock needlessly
        resembles rhubarb
        and umbrellas
*Along the river bank at Matlock by*
*the former quarries now colonised*
*by Sainsbury's*

    thistle islands
        moor in
           grazed grass
*C. arvensis. Beside the Tissington*
*Trail and in fields to either side,*
*most of the way to Buxton*

    buttercups are plentiful
        seeing as they taste
        so bad to sheep
*R. acris. In fields of ridge and furrow*
*where the lost village is between*
*Middleton and Gratton Dale*

HAIKU

dog rose &
  pussy willow
    getting along fine

dark-clustered
  merry shine
    with rain
*cherry*

gean, if I had
  your blossom
    I wouldn't chuck it away

meadowsweet smells
  of germaline
    & is nature's aspirin
*All around the packhorse bridge over the River Bradford where the Winster and Youlgreave roads separate*

flowers are made
  when it's time
    for sex

haiku by Alec Finlay | locations by Tony Baker

B
I
R
D
S

    the birds on the river
      aren't the same birds
        I dreamed on the river

    a pair of flyting magpies
      pay my polite 'morning'
        no attention

    sparrows arrow
      through the yard
        casting swift shadows


    the crows return
      to their brief night
        roosted in Hurt's Wood

    climbers mind
      your hand-
        holds for nests
    *ring ouzel*

    somewhere I can't see
      there are skirlock
        singing
    *skylark*


    startled dunlin
      scree open
        the moor's silence

    swifts dip in & out
      under the eaves
        of the Visitor Centre

    *yip yip yip*
      the blackbird
        darts about

HAIKU

where have all
  the swifts gone?

                    ordinary birds make
                        accomplished songsters
                              on the humdrum Moss

*teewit teewit tititi*
  little charmers
    at the teasel
*goldfinch*

as close as that
  to the dove
    I could've collared her

P
R
E
A
M
B
L
E

some colourful figures
are walking the hill
for me

soft form clouds
change their minds

meshed on the ridge
rambled places
come apart again

don't walk straight
when the path doesn't

set the stick on
swinging to &
fro & to

squeezed through
gap-tooth stones

you meet nice people
out walking
not gobshite chavs

such odd things
I think outdoors

walking backwards
or taking the path back
which breaks the spell?

cause + effect
shapes every dale

wetted the walking
map folds paper
into soft linen

if the river was straight
it would go on forever

sure of the way
the hiker thinks backwards
to where he left the map
where in the world
or wood are we?
with patches on
their gear
like dark clouds
once you're soaked
it doesn't matter
wherever we walk
it's in synthetic
+ merino socks
bringing the outdoors in
a pool by the umbrella
i'm so completely drained
what is it
with the second day?
as low as that
sky rationing our view
we keep walking
until the hill's virgule
takes us in
the miniscule's still capable
of a rhythmic bond
remembering Gerry laughing
when I said my legs
couldn't go that far
changing my steps
can only repeat

## white peak | dark peak

This catalogue is an open gate with paths leading to 70 poems – or *renga-view*, so named because they are composed in the traditional Japanese linked-verse form, *renga*, and each belongs to a place to see from, or to, a *view*.

Together the *renga-view* compose a *word-map* of the Peak District – a *word-map* is a descriptive poem of location.

You can experience the renga-view from *here*, in the catalogue, and as audio – via 20 QR-codes printed at the begining of this booklet and on the individual pages dedicated to each location. QR – Quick Response – is a matrix barcode that accesses the web via mobile phone technology. Camera-click, press your ear to the phone, hear the poem.

You can experience the renga-views *there*, on the **white peak | dark peak** website, *www.whitepeak-darkpeak.co.uk*, which displays the topographical poem typographically, with the lines laid-out to follow along the skylines which characterise the peak, tor, dale, hill or standing stone.

You can experience the renga-views in the field, by journeying to any of the 20 letterbox locations dispersed through the Peak District, where you can also collect the rubber stamp circle poem that each box contains. The audio is available in free download form, via QR-code plaques concealed within the letterboxes. Walk to the various views, stand where the poet stood, with the poem in your ear and the view before your eyes.

The work is an imaginative journey that may be taken from anywhere in the world; or a guided walk in the landscape – you choose: *here*, *there*, or a journey between the two.

Strange, isn't it, that we seldom read poems in their places: *Paterson* in Paterson, Oswald's *Dart* by that muddy river; odd, that Wordsworth's *For the spot where the hermitage stood on St Herbert's Island, Derwentwater,* is rarely read there, on that spot. When Basho and Sora tramped through the interior of Japan they went from view to view, wrote to the view, addressing landmarks – the rock at Sesshoseki oozing noxious fumes, surrounded by a halo of dead butterflies; the falls at Urami; the moon dripping on the pines at Shiogoshi – as so many travellers had before them. Along the way they stopped at villages and towns and composed renga, sharing tea and repartee.

I have practiced renga for a decade now, developing variants for mapping or collaborative shared writing. The accumulation of cultural images of the moors and dales of The Peak National Park seemed to invite a contemporary equivalent; a renewal in contemporary terms of poem-viewing as an everday activity, a flickr-like travelogue of images. **white peak** | **dark peak** was an experimental attempt to word-map an entire region. The first renga-views were composed on a rainy Sunday, June full moon, 2009 – the anniversary of Basho's arrival at the Shirakawa Barrier. That day he was too poorly to attend the nearby renga held in honour of his visit, so he sent Sora with a verse for the pot. I wasn't well enough to walk up Mam Tor, but I could still see the broken ridge out my window. We worked on through to Autumn, gathering new collaborators along the way, roaming from location to location, slowly making our way from the dark peak into the white.

Each of the poets walked, looked and wrote in their own way; some composing the poem along the path, step by step; others taking notes to recompose over time; some collaborating, others soloing; some in sensible gear, others hailed on, menaced by lightning; some led by the lamp of literature, others geographising. My own poems are compounds: *in situ* haiku, combined with phrases that I tracked down on hiking and climbing blogs, flickr photo-groups, enthusiastic folk-guides such as the *modern antiquarian*, and truffling through guidebooks – trusting the fidelity of those who loved these places. A poet is a radio.

The renga-view desire to double: go *there*, compose your own verses, each poem can expand exponentially. In an age in which plinths are crowded, bronze scarce, poetry proposes itself as the ideal form of public sculpture.

(AF)

### guides

There are 20 letterboxes, each connecting with a number of renga-view. To access the audio, scan the QR-code using the QR reader on your mobile phone, and follow the URL link to download the album. Each track listing begins with an Ordnance Survey SK reference, guiding you to the ideal viewpoint for the renga-view. Alternatively, the audio can be downloaded to any playback device, see *www.whitepeak-darkpeak.co.uk*, and listened to on location or at home.

The guides in this book give the location of each letterbox and the nearby viewpoints for the poems; in some cases they give a more detailed list of suggested viewpoints, referring to specific sections of the poems.

Each letterbox contains a rubber stamp circle poem, which may be stamped in the space provided.

## QR-code

Most current mobile phones have QR-code reader applications. Simply select the application on your device and take a snapshot of the QR-code, as you would with a normal camera.

For mobile phone devices that don't have this application, it is possible to download the QR-code reader for free from the internet. The following websites offer this service, as well as providing further information about QR technology.

*www.reader.kaywa.com*

*www.i-nigma.com*

*www.en.wikipedia.org/wiki/QR_Code*

*rubber stamp the circle poem here*

**Bleaklow**

LB: located in Torside Reservoir carpark
(53°28'54.41"N) (1°53'56.37"W)
SK 067983

**Coombes Clough | Alec Finlay**
From Crowden Brook carpark take the Pennine Way N SK 068991. The renga-views are from SK 066995 looking over Hollins Clough, Coombes Clough, Millstone Rocks & Lad's Leap; and S, from Lad's Leap SK 052998, looking over Torside & Rhodeswood Reservoirs.

**Shining Clough | Alec Finlay**
From the LB take the Longendale Trail E. Head S at the signpost to Wildboar Clough; keep the clough on your left. Cross the clough SK 082977 heading N and NE following the gritstone escarpment to the renga-view of the Dowstones SK 096987.

**Bleaklow (Higher Shelf Stones) | John Sewell**
Leave the Pennine Way at Devil's Dyke SK 094937. Head NW across the moor and Crooked Clough to Higher Shelf Stones SK 089948. This renga-view can be combined with the Wain Stones SK 093959 by continuing N.

**Bleaklow (Wain Stones) | Alec Finlay**
From the LB take the Longendale trail W to pick up the Pennine Way running S SK 057980. Follow the path to the Wain Stones SK 093959. Alternatively, complete the view of Higher Shelf Stones SK 089948 first, then head N.

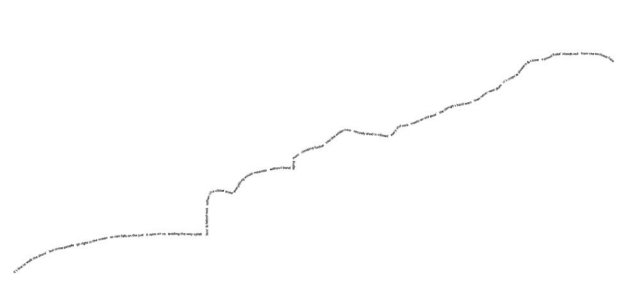

*rubber stamp the circle poem here*

Kinder North

LB: located opposite Birchen Clough Bridge carpark
(53°25'10.85"N) (1°50'12.76"W)
SK 109915

### Alport Dale | Martin Lucas
From Hayridge Farm SK 138896 head N following River Alport. At Alport Farm cross the river, heading E; then continue N/NW to the renga-view of Alport Castles SK 143915 and Birchin Hat SK 142916.

### Kinder North (Ashop Moor–Featherbed Moss–Seal Edge–Fairbrook Naze) | Alec Finlay
From the LB, follow the path S along Lady Clough. At River Ashop SK 107907 go W at the footbridge, heading onto Black Ashop Moor. Cross the footbridge at the ford SK 092906 and contour E, following the river on your left. At Gateside Clough SK116896 ascend onto the Edges and head W. Follow the Edges N to Fairbrook Naze SK 096897. To extend the view with Kinder South continue W to join the Pennine Way going S to Kinder Downfall SK 083889.

Field-recording: *River Ashop & River Alport (confluence)*, Bevis Bowden

*rubber stamp the circle poem here*

## Kinder South

LB: located in Barber Booth carpark
(53°21'33.78"N) (1°49'51.23"W)
SK 114847

### Kinder South (Kinder Downfall—Edale Moor—Crowden Brook) | Alec Finlay

From the LB take the path NW to join the Pennine Way at Upper Booth. Continue to Kinder Downfall SK 083889 where the renga-view begins. From here take the path E by SE to further views from Crowden Brook Falls SK 095873; to the SW lies Crowden Tower and the Woolpacks. From here descend through Crowden Clough back to the LB in Barber Booth.

Alternatively begin with Kinder North (Ashop Moor) heading W from Fairbrook Naze SK 096897 to join the Peninne Way going S to Kinder Downfall.

### Lepidoptera | Alec Finlay

The view describes sightings on Kinder Scout and Black Ashop Moor; combine the view with Kinder North and Kinder South.

*rubber stamp the circle poem here*

### Derwent & Ladybower

LB: located at Cutthroat Bridge
(53°22'57.92"N) (1°40'49.17"W)
SK 211874

### Derwent Edge | Ian Storr & Alec Finlay

The renga-view begins from along Derwent Edge, heading S. Keep on the track until you reach the view from Lead Hill SK 197874. Bear E to Cutthroat Bridge SK 214874.

### Derwent & Ladybower Reservoir | Alec Finlay

A circular renga-view starting and ending at Derwent Reservoir Dam SK 174896. Take the footpath N and follow the right fork up Walker's Clough SK 174908. At Shake Holes SK 182909 head S, keeping Pike Low on your right. From Briery Side SK 185894 continue S to the road, fork right, and head NW back to the Dam.

This view can be extended with Derwent Edge by turning left at the road and heading S; take the bridleway across Grindle Clough SK 190885 and then the footpath E to the crest of Derwent Edge SK 203880.

### Stanage Edge | Ian Storr & Alec Finlay

Begin from Moscar Lodge driveway SK 231878 and follow the edge path S. At the Long Causeway branch E to Stanedge Pole SK 246844 and then NE to Redmires Road, finishing beside the reservoir at SK 263858.

*rubber stamp the circle poem here*

## The Great Ridge

LB: located in Castleton carpark
(53°20'38.36"N) (1°46'38.39"W)
SK 149829

### The Great Ridge | Alec Finlay with Rebecca Hall
The first of two renga-views begin at Spring House Farm in Castleton SK 156841. Take the footpath N to the summit of Lose Hill SK 153853. Head SW along the ridge to Back Tor SK 145849.

### The Great Ridge (Back Tor) | Alec Finlay with Rebecca Hall
The second of two renga-views; from Back Tor SK 145849 continue on to Hollins Cross SK 136845. From here, go S to Mam Farm SK 134840 then SE along Odin Sitch to arrive in Castleton SK 147828.

### Rushup Edge | Alec Finlay
The renga-view describes the environs of Rushop Hall SK 095822; from the Pennine Bridleway walk NE along the footpath by the Hall, until you join the Sheffield Road that heads towards Castleton.

### Mam Tor: Transect | Laura Watts
Renga-view begins at the start of the collapsed A625. Follow the old road up to the Blue John car park, then turn north-west up the footpath to Mam Tor, pass the barrow, and then walk down the other side to Cold Side. Follow the footpath to Edale to the start of The Pennine Way.

Verse / GPS (OS) +/- 15m: 1 / SK 134 230; 2 / SK 134 150; 3 / SK 134 260; 4 / SK 132 250; 5 / SK 131 920; 6 / SK 132 010; 7 / SK 132 270; 8 / SK 132 360; 9 / SK 131 670; 10 / SK 131 680; 11 / SK 130 930; 12 / SK 128 610; 13 / SK 126 110; 14 / SK 125 160; 15 / SK125 010; 16 / SK 125 980; 17 / SK 125 580; 18 / SK 124 140; 19 / SK 124 030; 20 / SK 122 670.

### Cave Dale & Winnats Pass | Alec Finlay
Begin at Limestone Way in Castleton SK 151827, walking SW up Cave Dale. From here either return to Castleton and walk through Winnats Pass, or continue SW along the Limestone Way until you reach a crossroads SK 135813, then branch W then NW until you join the lane at Oxlow House. Follow the road E until you reach Winnats Pass Farm SK 130828 at the top of Winnats Pass.

### Blue John Cavern | Hamish Ironside
The renga-view is a tour of Blue John Cavern, located N of Winnats Pass SK 133831. Entrance fees apply.

### Speedwell Cavern | Hamish Ironside
The renga-view is a tour of Speedwell Cavern, entance is located on the road through Winnats Pass SK 139826. Entrance fees apply.

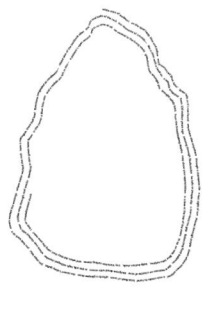
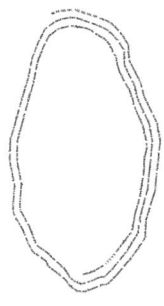

*rubber stamp the circle poem here*

Burbage Moor

LB: located in Surprise View carpark
(53°19'1.55"N) (1°37'24.24"W)
SK 251801

### Ox Stones | India McKellar & Alec Finlay

From the LB head N across the Mother Cap. When you reach the Rain Gauge SK 253815, head E to Carl Wark SK 258815 and continue E, across the footbridge over Burbage Brook, ascending onto Burbage Edge. Bear NE to Houndkirk Road SK 276816, then head N, across the moor, to the renga-view of the Ox Stones SK 280831.

This renga-view can be combined with Higger Tor and Carl Wark.

### Higger Tor | Alec Finlay & Ian Storr

The renga-view starts from the footpath at Toad's Mouth SK 261806 and heads N to the view of Higger Tor from the summit of Carl Wark SK 258815.

This renga-view can be extended into the nearby views of Carl Wark by continuing N to Higger Tor SK 257818. It can also be extended onto The Edges North by heading W from Carl Wark to Rain Gauge SK 253815 and then S to Millstone Edge SK 248807.

### Carl Wark | Alec Finlay

From the LB head N across the Mother Cap. When you reach the Rain Gauge SK 253815, head E to Carl Wark SK 258815 and then N to Higger Tor SK 257818, from where the renga-view is composed.

*rubber stamp the circle poem here*

## The Edges North

LB: located in Hay Wood carpark
(53°17′45.31″N) (1°37′5.01″W)
SK 257777

### Yarncliff Wood | Alec Finlay

The renga-view describes Yarncliff Wood SK 253792. From the LB take the footpath N through Hay Wood, into Nether Padley. When you reach the B6521, cross the road and take the footpath SK 252787, just N of Grindleford Station, leading into Yarncliffe Woods. Alternatively, park at the station, cross the railway line, and take the path to the right, in front of Burbage Brook SK 251788.

### Woods | Alec Finlay

This renga-view describes typical Peak District woodland, such as Yarncliff Wood, Oxhay Wood, Bretton Clough, Manners Wood.

### The Edges North (Millstone Edge–The Pinnacle) | Alec Finlay

The first of two renga-views proceeds S from Millstone Edge.

Millstone Edge SK 248807; Padley Woods & Burbage Brook SK 252785.

### The Edges North (Millstone Edge–The Pinnacle) | Alec Finlay

The second renga-view begins from Froggatt Edge SK 250770; Stoke Flats SK 256765; The Pinnacle SK 250763 and Bees Wood. Extend the view with The Edges South by continuing S from The Pinnacle and onto Curbar Edge SK 253758.

These two renga-views can be extended with The Edges South.

### Waterfall Swallet | John Sewell

This renga-view is of Waterfall Swallet SK 199771.

### Eyam | Judy Kendall with John Sewell

The renga-view begins at Town End in Eyam village SK 221765 and heads W through the village to St Lawrence's SK 216765 and Cucklet Delf SK 215764.

Field-recording: *Burbage Brook*, Bevis Bowden

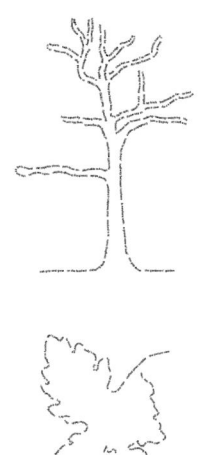

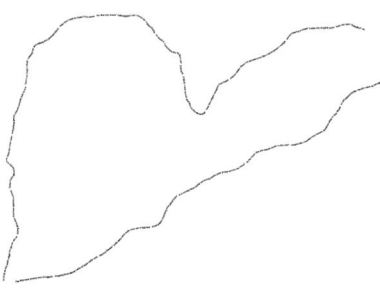

*rubber stamp the circle poem here*

## The Edges South

LB: located in Birchen Edge carpark
(53°14'43.36"N) (1°34'54.38"W)
SK 281722

### The Edges South (Curbar Edge–Birchen Edge) | Alec Finlay

This series of renga-views proceeds S from Curbar Edge, see also The Edges North.

Curbar Edge SK 253758; Swine Sty SK 271750; Baslow Edge SK 260746; view Gardom Edge from the Wellington Monument SK 264737; Bar Brook & Kitty Lockyer's Garden SK 267735; view Birchen Edge from near the Three Men SK 274726.

### The Edges South (The Eagle Stone) | Alec Finlay

Eagle Stone SK 263738; with views to Baslow Hall to the SW from Baslow Edge.

### Curbar Edge | Martin Lucas

Start at Curbar Edge carpark SK 261746 and head NW along Curbar Edge.

### River Derwent | Alec Finlay

Renga-view of the Derwent.

### Chatsworth | Alan Halsey & Geraldine Monk

Renga-view of Chatsworth House garden and park, seen from Stand Wood SK 269704. Entrance fees apply.

Field-recording: *Ivy Bar Brook*, Bevis Bowden

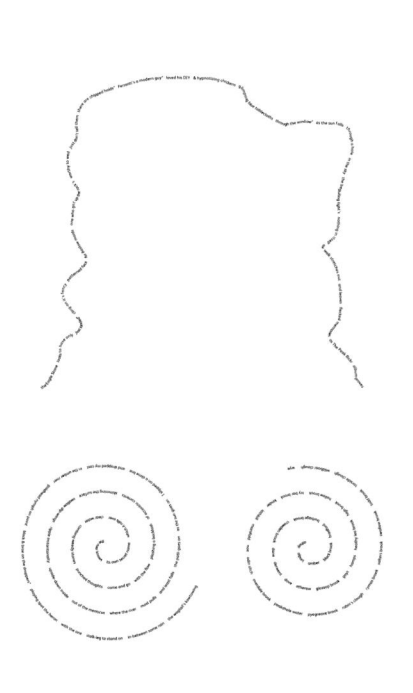

*rubber stamp the circle poem here*

## Monsal Dale

LB: located in Monsal Head carpark
(53°14'24.89"N) (1°43'28.90"W)
SK 185716

### Cressbrook Dale & Water-Cum-Jolly | John Sewell
Take the footpath behind Cressbrook Mill SK 173727. Cross the R. Wye and follow the footpath north climbing above the dale to meet the Monsal Trail. Take in the renga-view SK 167727, above the railway trackbed. The view can be extended with Monsal Dale Viaduct & Fin Cop, by continuing along the Monsal Trail to Monsal Head SK 185716.

### Monsal Dale | Alec Finlay
Renga-view of Fin Cop from Monsal Head and the aqueduct SK 185716.

### Peter's Stone, Ravensdale | India McKellar & Alec Finlay
Take the footpath W from Wardlow Mires SK 180755 to Peter's Stone SK 174754. Follow the footpath S as far as Ravensdale Cottages SK 173736.

*rubber stamp the circle poem here*

### Monk's Dale

LB: located in Miller's Dale carpark
(53°15'22.46"N) (1°47'42.32"W)
SK 137734

### Monk's Dale | Alec Finlay

From the LB exit left out of Miller's Dale carpark. Take the footpath that begins on the sharp left bend in the road SK 139734. Follow the path across the stream and take the Limestone Way N above Monk's Dale. At the road turn W and return via Monk's Dale.

### Chee Dale | Judy Kendall

The renga-view begins from the LB heading W along the R. Wye to Chee Tor SK 124733.

### Ravenstor | Alec Finlay

From the LB take the Monsal Trail E along the R. Wye. There are good views of Ravenstor in and around SK 150730.

The view can be extended with Chee Dale by continuing W along the R. Wye to the LB at Miller's Dale carpark.

### Deepdale & Backdale | David Troupes

From Wye Dale carpark (off of the A6) SK 104725, cross the road taking the footpath S. Branch SW into Deepdale for the start of the renga-view SK 097713 and head E along the Midshires Way, with views of Chelmerton Low to the N SK 114703.

*rubber stamp the circle poem here*

## Combs Moss

LB: located in Chapel-en-le-Frith Station carpark
(53°18'44.08"N) (1°55'6.70"W)
SK 055795

**Combs Moss (Castle Naze–Flint Cough)** | Alec Finlay
From the LB, cross the railway and head W parallel to the railway line. Then track S through Bank Hall Farm to Cowlow Lane SK 053786, Cowlow and Lady Low are on either side of the road. Ascend the track opposite Bank Hall to the top of Castle Naze SK 054784. Pygreave wood and the tumuli are immediately below. Head S along Combs Edge; Flint Clough and Buxton lie to the S.

circle poem, after Arne Naess

*rubber stamp the circle poem here*

Goyt's Moss

LB: located at Peak View Tea Rooms
(53°15'0.59"N) (2° 0'18.38"W)
SK 997726

**Shining Tor (Thursbitch–Cat Tor–Pym Chair–Windgather Rocks)** | Mark Rutter
The first of two renga-views, best combined with the connected views of Shining Tor & Windgather Rocks. From the LB, continue NE along the access road to Stake Farm SK 001728 and pick up the path N, then branching NW to the summit of Shining Tor SK 995736. Continue N along the ridge, passing above Thursbitch to the W SK 996753 and ascending Cats Tor SK 995759. Then head N to Pym Chair SK 996767.

**Shining Tor & Windgather Rocks** | Alec Finlay
The second of two renga-views (see Shining Tor). The view describes the summit of Shining Tor from Pym Chair SK 996767 and then proceeds N to Windgather Rocks SK 995785.

**Shutlingsloe (Shutlingsloe–Wildboarclough–Panniers Pool)** | Alec Finlay
Begin from the path SW of Clough House carpark SK 986698. Follow the path S into Wildboar Clough; when you reach the road go right and take the next footpath on your left, to Berry Bank SK 984683. From here go left, heading N until you reach the road. Continue right and take the next footpath left SK 991686. Keep following the footpath, across the A54, to Cuthorn SK 004682, before contouring NE passed Three Shire Heads to Pannier's Pool SK 009685.

circle poem, after Arne Naess

Field-recording: *River Goyt*, Bevis Bowden

*rubber stamp the circle poem here*

### The Roaches

LB: located near Roaches Gate, close to
The Roaches carpark, Roach Road
(53° 9'23.39"N) (1°59'40.38"W)
SK 004621

**Gib Torr Rocks – Black Brook Nature Reserve –
Goldsitch Moss – Gib Torr | Alec Finlay**
The renga-view is from Gib Torr Rock SK 017647 and
the surrounding Black Brook Nature Reserve, looking
E to Goldsitch Moss and Gib Torr.

**Gradbach – Lud's Church – Back Dane| Alec Finlay**
The first of two renga-views; from the carpark near
Manor Farm SK 998662, take the footpath SW along
the river, crossing the footbridge over Black Brook
to ascend to Lud's Church SK 986656 where the
renga-view begins. From here go W, before swinging
E along a ridge track SK 977655. The Hanging Stone
is to the W. Follow the ridge track E, passing above
Lud's Church, and pick up the path which heads SE
to the track before Bearstone Rocks SK 995645.

**Bearstone Rock – Roach End – Five Clouds –
The Roaches – Doxey Pool | Alec Finlay**
The second renga-view begins from the track at
Bearstone Rocks SK 995645 and continues S to
The Roaches SK 002638 and Doxey Pool SK 004627.
Extend this view with Hen Cloud by continuing SE to
the base of Hen Cloud SK 007620.

**Hen Cloud | Alec Finlay**
From the LB head to the foot of Hen Cloud SK 007619,
contouring E to Well Farm SK 009620. Continue SE,
crossing the stream before heading N under

Ferny Knowl SK 015617. Continue N to Blue Hills
SK 016626; Ramshaw Rocks lie to the E.

Field-recording: *River Dane*, Bevis Bowden

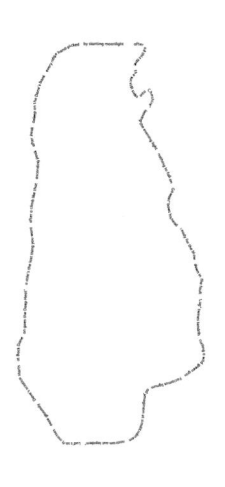

Trousers steps out*
of the stage's median
onto The Hanging Stone

beating grouse
nip over Reach End

piercing the sky
cliff's repeat
incised spurs

hanging half ropes
like streamers

If I climb on hour
I need to rest for those*
as I take it slow

winding the syncline
down corrugated cliffs

steps along the whaleback
take us via the Roaches
that boulder's a snail*

the wallabies* are gone
from the Sloth* & Swan
ninepegg ring

hung upside down
for 55 years

look at that view
stretching a beauty*

Rockhall now Fuckall
King Doug's windows*
boarded to the west

naked spooks crag-rats*
fiddle for chalk

pink grit tiers
hover clouds over
the edge like Ra's*

Peely, whose says
Doxey's undies?*

*rubber stamp the circle poem here*

## The Dragon's Back

LB: located on Earl Sterndale Green
(53°12'0.38"N) (1°51'58.73"W)
SK 090671

### The Dragon's Back (Parkhouse Hill & Chrome Hill) | Laura Watts

Renga-view begins at The Quiet Woman in Earl Sterndale. Follow the footpath west towards Parkhouse Hill, then curve around the base of the hill, and up the ridge of Chrome Hill. The walk ends at the tail of Chrome Hill.

Verse / GPS (OS) +/- 15m: 1 / SK 089 670; 2 / SK 087 310; 3 / SK 086 260; 4 / SK 085 680; 5 / SK 085 670; 6 / SK 083 850; 7 / SK 082 760; 8 / SK 080 750; 9 / SK 078 640; 10 / SK 077 760; 11 / SK 076 740; 12 / SK 074 890; 13 / SK 074 300; 14 / SK 073 670; 15 / SK 072 980; 16 / SK 071 900; 17 / SK 071 150; 18 / SK 070 570; 19 / SK 069 710; 20 / SK 069 700.

### Dowel Dale | Alec Finlay

The view describes a walk through Dowel Dale. Begin from the path S of Harley Grange SK 084677 and head W to the road at Dowel Dale SK 076678.

### High Wheeldon | Andrew Shimield

The renga-view begins from the bridleway at Top o' th' Edge SK 091651. Follow the path NE over Beggar's Bridge SK 094656 towards High Wheeldon; ascend to the summit SK 101662. Earl Sterndale and The Quiet Woman lie to the NW. Extend the view with Parkhouse Hill & Chrome Hill by heading N to The Quiet Woman SK 090670.

This renga-view can be extended with the nearby view of Pilsbury Castle by heading SE into Crowdicote and picking up the Salt Way at Bridge End Farm SK 103649

### Pilsbury Castle | Alec Finlay

Take the Salt Way in Crowdicote, Bridge End Farm SK 103649, heading SE to Pilsbury Castle SK 114640. Continue S, then take the right-branch track S into Pilsbury. Take the footpath SW SK 117634 across the R. Dove with the view ahead to Sheen Hill.

*rubber stamp the circle poem here*

## Lathkill Dale

LB: located at Conksbury Bridge
(53°11'14.87"N) (1°41'3.19"W)
SK 213657

### Lathkill Dale (Mill Farm–One Ash Grange) | Linda France

The renga-view begins at the footpath by Mill Farm SK 181664, heading S to the Lathkill. At the river head W, cross Sheepwash Bridge SK 174655 and go S to meet the Limestone Way. From here head W to One Ash Grange SK 169653. Extend the view with the nearby renga-views of Lathkill Dale (Carter's Mill–Over Haddon), Calling Low Dale & Cales Dale SK 174655.

### Lathkill Dale (Carter's Mill–Over Haddon) | Linda France

The renga-view begins at Carters Mill SK 195650, E of which is a footbridge leading to Thomas Bateman's House. Continue E along the Lathkill to the packhorse bridge SK 204662, leading into Over Haddon and St Anne's Church SK 204664. Extend this view with the nearby renga-views of Lathkill Dale (Mill Farm–One Ash Grange), Calling Low Dale & Cales Dale SK 174655.

### Cales Dale | Alec Finlay

Calling Low Dale joins Lathkill Dale at SK 184657; Cales Dale joins Lathkill Dale at SK 174655.

### Arbor Low | Linda France

The renga-view is of Arbor Low SK 160635 and Gib Hill.

### Minninglow–High Peak Trail–Roystone Rocks | Alec Finlay

The renga-view is of Minninglow, NE of the public access track SK 205573, heading SW to Roystone Rocks.

Field-recording: *River Lathkill*, Bevis Bowden

*rubber stamp the circle poem here*

## Stanton Moor

LB: located in carpark on Birchover Road,
opposite Birchover Stone
(53° 9'32.38"N) (1°38'27.54"W)
SK 241624

### Castle Ring | Judy Kendall with Alec Finlay & John Sewell
Park at Youlgreave village; the renga-view of Castle Ring mostly follows the Youlgreave stretch of the Limestone Way SK 218630. Extend the walk with the view of Limestone Way from Castle Ring SK 218630.

### The Limestone Way (Castle Ring) | Judy Kendall with Alec Finlay & John Sewell
Start from Castle Ring SK 218630, with Youlgreave to the N and Black Nursery Plantation to the SW. Continue S, passing Harthill Farm to Robin Hood Stride SK 225624.

### Stanton Moor (Birchover–Nine Ladies–Stanton Moor) | Alec Finlay with Rebecca Hall
This series of renga-views is a circular walk beginning from the footpath at Lees Road SK 46625. Head NE passing the Tower Cairn SK 252634. Continue N to The Nine Ladies SK 249636. From here, walk S across the moor, passing the quarries on your right. Continue S until you reach the Cork Stone SK 244627, then head SE to rejoin Lees Road. The view can be extended with Cork Stone & Andle Stone.

### Stanton Moor (Cork Stone) | Alec Finlay
The view describes the Cork Stone SK 244627 on Stanton Moor, N of the LB. Extend the view with Andle Stone SK 240629 on your way back.

### Stanton Moor (Andle Stone) | Alec Finlay
The view describes the Andle Stone, located on the W side of the Birchover Road, SK 240629. It can be combined with nearby views of the Cork Stone and Stanton Moor.

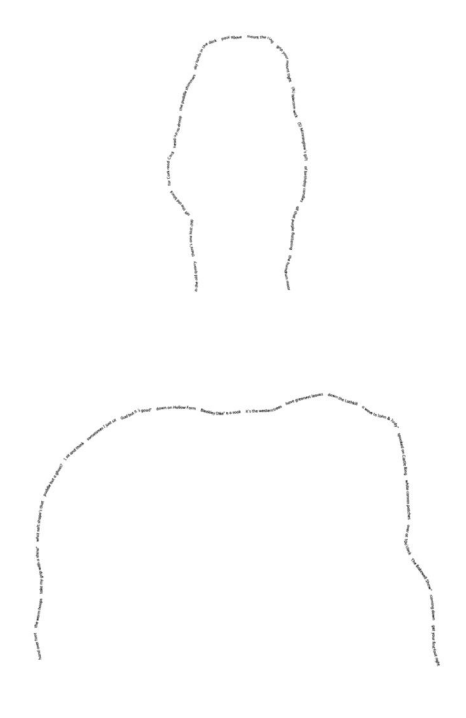

*rubber stamp the circle poem here*

## Two Dales

LB: Tax Farm Cottages (Farley Lane)
(53° 9'56.75"N) (1°33'43.30"W)
SK 294633

**Sydnope Hall (Two Dales) | Alan Halsey
& Geraldine Monk**

To reach the LB, park on Farley Lane, above Tax Farm SK 295629 and take the footpath opposite to Tax Farm Cottages. From the LB continue along the footpath, bearing NE along Sydnope Brook and crossing the footbridge to Sydnope Hall Farm SK 290639. From here you can track E towards the Hall before looping back down to the Brook.

*rubber stamp the circle poem here*

### Milldale

LB: located in Alstonefield carpark
(53° 5'51.93"N) (1°48'23.24"W)
SK 131556

### Wolfscote Dale | Alec Finlay & Tony Baker

From the LB, take the bridleway NE from Lode Lane SK 135657. The renga-view begins from Coldeaton Bridge SK 146562, heading N along the R. Dove into Wolfscote Dale as far as Frank in th' Rocks Bridge SK 130584. The view can be extended with Alstonefield by crossing Frank in th' Rocks Bridge and following the track S between Gratton and Narrowdale Hill, to join the path near Low Plantation SK 126565.

### Alstonefield | Alec Finlay, after Peter Riley

The renga-view is of the village of Alstonefield, descending S from the path near Low Plantation SK 126565.

### Milldale & Viator Bridge | Alan Halsey & Geraldine Monk

From the LB take the path SE off Millway Lane SK 134554. The renga-view is of Viator Bridge SK 148546 looking S to Dove Dale and N to Milldale.

Field-recording: *River Dove*, Bevis Bowden

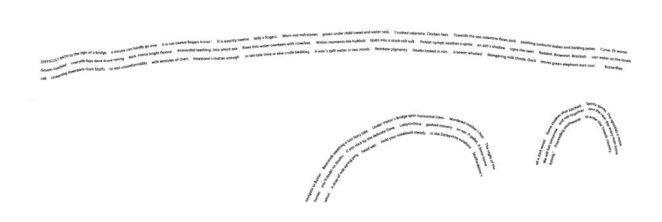

*rubber stamp the circle poem here*

### Dovedale

LB: located at Ilam Hall
(53° 3'11.27"N) (1°48'17.76"W)
SK 132506

### Thorpe Cloud | Alec Finlay
From the LB walk into Ilam village for the renga-view NE towards Thorpe Cloud. Extend the renga-view with the view to Bunster Hill and a walk into Dovedale.

### Hill Farmer (Bunster Hill) | Alec Finlay
From the LB walk into Ilam village for the renga-view N towards Bunster Hill. Extend the renga-view with the view to Thorpe Cloud and a walk into Dovedale.

### Dovedale | Ann Atkinson & River Wolton
The renga-view begins from Dovedale carpark SK 146509 and follows the Dove to Reynard's Cave SK 145525 and back. This renga-view can be extended with Ilam Rock by continuing N along the Dove.

### Ilam Rock | David Cobb
The renga-view begins from Reynard's Cave SK 145525 and continues N to Ilam Rock SK 143532. It can be combined with the nearby renga-views of Dovedale, Bunster Hill and Thorpe Cloud.

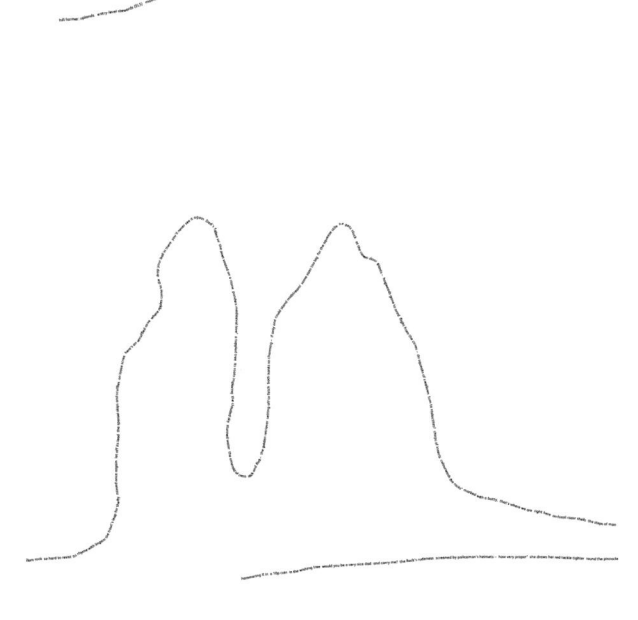

*rubber stamp the circle poem here*

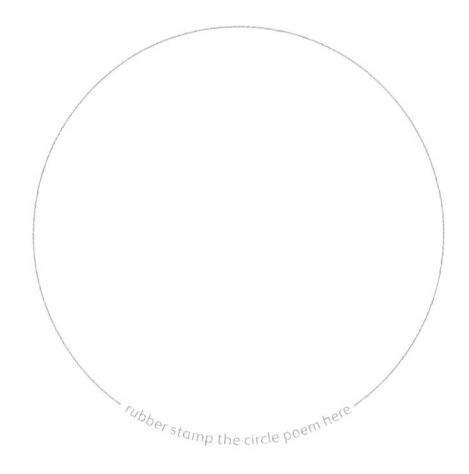

### Thor's Cave

LB Wetton carpark
(53° 5'36.70"N) (1°50'18.87"W)
SK 108552

### Thor's Cave | John Sewell

This renga-view describes the view from Thor's Cave towards Ossom's Hill and from there back towards the cave. Take the NW path to Leek Road. At SK 106553 take the footpath W/SW down the dale. In the wood, a footpath left accesses the cave. Continue down, cross the R. Manifold. Turn right onto the cycle trail for the renga-view of Thor's Cave SK 097549.

Field-recording: *River Manifold*, Bevis Bowden

                    dark       on
                  white       night
                    in      daylight
                grey dawn and dusk
               between    harnessed in, bluff
              to bluff     the river ricochets a
              pinball course       around a bend
              suddenly       it's raised there, an open
           mouth      mirroring years   subwith
           crowskilt and meadowsweet,    hornbell
          limestone-niched within    a Chatsworth,
          boiling    its entrance: a misplaced piece of
          closey cuts    not to puddled mud, the blissfold
          ripples through poplar leaves      four hundred rising
         moon   through hazels, take you back    ten thousand
         years    who'd choose to face the entrance world up
         a scramble, with mud-slicked soles   this maw could
         still pay      seven red floodmasters,    still gape for
         more    head to head, nothing     and everything
         endlessly changing    dark on white     between
         dusk and dawn    grey daylight in night    a lancet
          side lights the crossing    Deanie Hill glances back
          at you    breath well and truly whisked,    the cave
          mouth closing    as it nips you down    not
           so much a floor anymore    as a slippery of
           marble    they borrowed not deep clays    and
            gravels, flamed the floor clean    for one
            Roman coin     leaping the cave-lid    froun,
              hyaena, rhinestein and lemming    chisp
               of elk bone    palaeolithic curses, stones
                rocks from but there pot    trying-aches,
                 every where large        unsyncopated
                   plinking, drip-plops       i knew where
                    i'd sleep    that kissed-lidk chamber
                      where clay'r     just clay, not
                        mud       nothing head to
                          head   and everything
                             endlessly changing.

## bibliography

Tim Atkins, *Horace* (O Books, 2007)

Russell P. O. Beach & Rebecca Snelling, *Peak District: Ordnance Survey Leisure Guide* (AA Publishing, 1987)

Roy Christian, *The Peak District* (David & Charles, 1976)

Brian Conduit & Kevin Borman, *Peak District Walks* (Jarrold, 1989)

Trevor Brighton, *The Discovery of the Peak District, from Hades to Elysium* (Phillimore, 2004)

Charles Cotton & Izaak Walton, *The Compleat Angler* (Coachwhip Publications, 2005)

Henry Corbin, trans. by Nancy Pearson, *The Man of light in Iranian Sufism* (Random House, 1978)

Hunter Davies, *The Best of Wainwright* (Frances Lincoln, 2004)

Michael Drayton, *The Complete Works of Michael Drayton*, vo. 1, Polyolbion (Adamant Media Corporation, 2001)

K. C. Edwards, *The Peak District* (Fontana New Naturalist, 1962)

John Felstiner, *Paul Celan: Poet, Survivor, Jew* (Yale University Press, 2001)

Trevor D. Ford, *Rocks & Scenery of the Peak District* (Landmark Publishing, 2006)

Ron & Marlene Freethy, *Discovering the Pennines* (John Donald, 1992)

Hamish Fulton, *Hamish Fulton* (Richter, 2001)

R. Murray Gilchrist, *The Peak District* (Blackie & Son, c. 1910)

John Gilmour & Max Walters, *Wild Flowers* (Fontana New Naturalist, 1972)

Geofrey Grigson, *The Englishman's Flora* (Phoenix House, 1960)

Mike Harding, *Walking the Peak and Pennines* (Michael Joseph, 1992)

Simon Harrap, *RSPB Guide to British Birds* (Helm, 2007)

David Hinton, trans., *Mountain Home: The Wilderness Poetry of Anceint China* (Anvil, 2007)

F. Philip Holland, *Words of the White Peak: the Disappearing Dialect of a Derbyshire Village* (Anecdotes Publishing, 2008)

Tony Hopkins, *The Peak District* (AA Publishing, 1996)

Rev. Joseph Hunter, *The Hallamshire Glossary* (University of Sheffield, 1983)

Geoffrey Hutchings, *Landscape Drawing* (Methuen, 1960)

Jack Kerouac, *some of the dharma* (Viking, 1997)

David McAleavey, *Huge Haiku* (Chax press, 2005)

John. N. Merrill, *The Limey Way* (J. N. M., 1983)

John. N. Merrill, *The Peakland Way* (J. N. M., 1983)

Roy Millward & Adrian Robinson, *The Peak District* (Eyre Methuen, 1975)

Patrick Monkhouse, *Peak District National Park* (HMSO, 1960)

John Morrison et al., *50 Walks in the Peak District* (AA Publishing, 2008)

Paul Muldoon, *Moy Sand and Gravel* (Faber & Faber, 2002)

Arne Naess, *The Ecology of Wisdom: Writings* (Counterpoint, 2008)

Lorine Niedecker, *Collected Works* (Univeristy of California, 2002)

Gerrit Noordzij, *The Stroke* (Hyphen Press, 2005)

Paul Nunn, *Rock Climbing in the Peak District* (Constable, 1975)

John & Anne Nuttall, *Peak District* (Ward Lock, 1994)

W. H. Pearsall, *Mountains & Moorlands* (Collins, 1950)

Lindsey Porter, *Southern Peak District* (Landmark Publishing, 1999)

W. A. Poucher, *The Peak & Pennines* (Constable, 1983)

Anthony Poulton-Smith, *Derbyshire Place-Names* (Sutton Publishing, 2005)

John Ramsbottom, *Mushrooms & Toadstools* (New Naturalist Series, Collins, 1953)

Rodger Refern, *Peak District Diary* (Sigma Leisure, 1992)

Mark Richards, *High Peaks Walks* (Cicerone Press, 1982)

Mark Richards, *The Northern Dales* (Cicerone Press, 1985)

Mark Richards, *The Southern Dales, White Peak Walks* (Cicerone Press, 1988)

Peter Riley, *Alstonefield* (Carcanet, 2003)

Francis Rose, *The Wildflower Key* (Frederick Warne, 2006)

Roly Smith, *Peak District: Collins Rambler's Guide* (Harper Collins, 2000)

Roly Smith, *Peak District: Photographic Memories of Britain* (Frith brook Company, 2003)

Gordon Stainforth, *The Climber as Visionary: Rock climbing in the Peak District*

John Stevens, trans., *Mountain Tasting: Zen Haiku by Santoka Taneda* (Weatherhill, 1980)

John Sewell, *Hokusai's 21 Glimpses of Skiddaw*

Rebecca Solnit, *Storming the gates of paradise* (Univeristy of California, 2007)

Soiku Shigematsu, trans., *A Zen Forest* (Weatherhill, 1981)

Ian Stephen, *Adrift* (Periplum, 2007)

Rob Talbot and Robin Whiteman, *The Peak District* (Weidenfeld & Nicolson, 1997)

Makoto Ueda, *Basho and his Interpreters: Selected Hokku with Commentary, Makoto Ueda* (Stanford University Press, 1992)

Burton Watson, trans., *Masaoka Shiki: Selected Poems* (Columbia University Press, 2007)

Burton Watson, trans., *Taneda Santoka: For all my walking* (Columbia University Press, 2003)

White Watson, *Delineation of the Strata of Derbyshire* (W. Todd, 1811)

Charles Wildgoose, *Waterside Walks in the Peak District* (Countryside Books, 2008)

**websites**

www.peakdistrict.gov.uk

www.peakwalks.blogspot.com

www.walkingenglishman.com/peakdistrict

www.derbyshirefishingblog.blogspot.com

www.themodernantiquarian.com

www.flickr.com/groups/peakdistrict

www.flickr.com/groups/derbyshire_grp

www.flickr.com/photos/primed_minister

www.markrichards.info

www.peakdistrictonline.co.uk

www.ncl.ac.uk/hydroinformatics

**maps**

Ordnance Survey Explorer Map, OL1 (2006)

Ordnance Survey Explorer Map, OL24 (2008)

Ordnance Survey Travel Map, Tour 4 (2007)

AA Pictorial Map, Peak District

Google Earth

white peak | dark peak

published in an edition of 750 copies for *re : place*, a programme of site-specific contemporary visual arts commissions across Derbyshire, 2009–2011, curated by David Gilbert

copyright © Alec Finlay, the authors, the artists 2010

The artist wishes to give especial thanks to the key contributors to the project, David Gilbert, John Sewell, Rebecca Hall and Caroline Smith; grateful thanks to all the poets who took part; thanks also to Lucy Richards and Richy Lamb (StudioLR); Bill Bevan (Peak District National Park); Jim Horsfall, Ann Atkinson, Tony Baker, David Cobb, Paul Conneally, Cath Gilbert, Alan Halsey, Hamish Ironside, Judy Kendall, Martin Lucas, India McKellar, Geraldine Monk, Mark Rutter, Andrew Shimield, Ian Storr, David Troupes, Laura Watts, River Wolton, Harry Gilonis, Colin Sackett, Mark Richards, Lee Turner (Hole Editions), Jim Hare, and the Wirksworth Festival.

morning star
studio alec finlay, 36 Lime Street, Newcastle-upon-Tyne

Derbyshire Arts Development Group
re : place, Newell Cottage, Main Street, Birchover, Derbyshire

designed by Alec Finlay & StudioLR
printed by Allander, Edinburgh

ISBN 978-1904477099